Solo with Grazing Deer

David Wevill

TORONTO

Exile Editions
2001

This edition is published by Exile Editions Limited,
20 Dale Avenue, Toronto, Ontario, Canada   M4W 1K4

SALES DISTRIBUTION:
McArthur & Company
c/o Harper Collins
1995 Markham Road
Toronto, ON
M1B 5M8
toll free:
1 800 387 0117
1 800 668 5788 (fax)

Design and Composition by TIM HANNA
Cover Art Zero Weather
Typeset at MOONS OF JUPITER
Printed and Bound by AGMV MARQUIS

The publisher wishes to acknowledge
the assistance toward publication of the Canada Council
and the Ontario Arts Council.

ISBN 1-55096-640-5

*Presence is just a special case
in the category of absence.*
— ROBERTO CALASSO, KA

*Deer graze here each morning,
for you harm nothing.*
— TU FU

Contents

THE RIVER THAT DROWNED

Years ago when I was a child in Japan
there were no seasons I can remember.
There were always soldiers in the streets
and children wore black uniforms to school.

In our high garden above the valley
of small houses, I was at home. There
were Christmases, the birth of a sister
parties with paper hats, lawn tennis, skiing

in the winter mountains. By then
the armies were deep in China, towns were burning.
I remember helping the gardener, my friend
wind the khaki cloth puttees around his shins

before he went off to drill in a dusty field
below the house. I was at war
with no one, only the English neighbour boy
who'd come to play and hogged my favourite toys.

There are films my father made recording
some of this. I rescued what I could
of the old 16mm reels, cracked, spliced and
faded, and had them compressed to a brief

video memento. The wide-eyed child my self
survives there in a world his parents remembered
too fondly to ever feel quite whole again
in the deeper snows of Canada we came to

before the armies moved south out of China
before the murders in Asia, the bombs on
Hawaii, the killings back westward across
the islands, the last incredible fires.

LAMP

While I was dreaming inside my flame
the wind bit at the edges of my teeth
and I thought I could see in the dark—
it was your word against mine.

Though they had broken shattered pieced together
Dresden and Hiroshima
Coventry London Guernica
the shadows you left wouldn't move.

So in Robert Capa's photograph
of a street in Bilbao in 1936
eight women and men and a young girl
look up at the sky at where German bombers

are coming. So it might have been
a little before dawn when a boy not quite one
woke up in a white crib in Yokohama
and saw shadows cross the ceiling of his room

—the world had soft bones
and old and brittle bones
and from time to time the light falls
exactly where the body runs to hide.

SABI

I feel my rust beginning.
It is inside me and between my fingers
a slow cold itching, like distant rain.
Or brown eating at the edge of a leaf
which is the light withdrawing
the mirror withheld
the air's child that hides.

The sun tests the future with a tentative hand.
I know the gender of water, the cold
beginning of memory under the long evening light
that comes to no fulfillment but itself.
The light that keeps returning has no language.
I am content to remember how you breathed.

MEMORY AND SEASON

Somewhere between here and Japan, the summer wind rises
as delicate as a salad made by her hands.
It was a loss of heart we were thinking about
when pain killed the child too far away.
How often, brother, lying under the stars
you have returned to now, how often and
in all fairness did her soft cry warn us
too soon or too late?

RUNE

Under the wind there is a place where you can hide.
Think of it as a silent event. An evening comes,
and you are ready to tell a story you have never
heard, tell it in such a way that whatever secrets
you had gather around you now to listen. They have
no name but yours, and they are still listening.

THE HIGH COLD AIR

My brother, there are just
bones under the skin, as if
air had entered and dried up
the rest of him. As if
the driest of winds had cracked through
and stolen the water
so he died of thirst
not cancer, but thirst

So what of this skeleton leaf
gone but for the thin pattern of veins

And the girl they call Juanita
under that high mountain ice
kept preserved, knees
to chin, neck bent, eyes gone
what name can bring her to life
can comb her long hair with its hand
whisper that life is good
so good?

LANDSCAPE

In autumn the silences grow loud.
The sounds become echoes.
I have been gone a long time, they
changed my number, the branch
I hung from has been cut.
In the room the shadow dolls
play across bare walls, there are
fresh spiders. The music I heard came
from outdoors, celebrations of air, wind
rain, at the ear's edges, listening.
Why won't you come in? A traffic
of handcars running along rails over
loose coals. An engine starting stops
abruptly. The silence is like a brush across
dry canvas, like slow fingers playing
through pubic hair. A white cat sits
like a harp on the window sill. It is
cold in the mountains, after a summer
training my eyes to see
what they once remembered. I note
the place where my chair stood
a square of pale light on the grey
carpet. What would you like to do?
The soup kitchen, the popular *sushi* bar
usually fill by noon. The river
below is the colour and chill
of fish, my fingers go numb
winding and unwinding this wet string.

You used to play an elegant piano.
Now in the place where the piano was
a crowd of echoes cries circling
desperately to find your hands. We are
out of touch. A sudden dash of rain
wets the glass and moves on. Tires
in the street exhale through wet teeth.
You were impatient with me. Three
seasons out of four the room chose colours
we both liked, heights of canyons brushed
with a first snow, brown shadowed by deep
green in the conifers just before dawn.
The patch of shadow where night
lay still in your armpit, a smell
like riverweed a moment out of water.
The almost white room is
emptying now. It is a book with blank pages
or a book whose familiar pages have faded
to this. There is no eloquence like
whiteness and silence. There are no
words where words end. The
room is empty now and white with shadows.
Black forest against white mountains
far away. A lone crow flying.

REVENANT

Too far within the eye
the smell of conifer wind, hot summer wood.

To outlive your childhood
the needy flies, the knee-deep water
rivering over the heads of soft stones.

Give a thought to the age
of things I've touched, always
the blessing of forgetfulness

in the heat of the city
the captive memory wind killing time.

Or there is what doesn't use its hands
to lift itself. Out of the chilled stream
into her young rose mouth
opening like numbers. Lost

moments, opportunities. The
names of some gone to seed in their lives
as I have (you have) mine.

What I see can only stretch beyond itself
into the shadows of futures
as things were then. The
sunlight feels closer now

because the only shadow is mine.
It took all those years to get here.

MAY MONTH

For Isabela

Why do I feel suddenly happy?
I must have been happy all along, and didn't know it.
Is this possible?

Of the homes I have abandoned.
There are trees that never see the sun
but they carry the memory of suns.

Out of the grass steps a bird with no wings.

The youngest one here
blows out two candles.

Her voice is only a breath. Between
two wishes a scar grows over an old wound
as gentle as an eye approaching evening.

Whish! the bird has flown.

BLUE ROOFS

Antlers of white cloud
high to the north.
Bands of winter.

I remember one thing I should not
have forgotten. White times two,
an absence of mind.

Thinking to understand what cost her
her life, abstractions
of distance now, haiku

spelling their way from the sun
into my open hand,
rain snow snow

beginnings of blue.
Somewhere, how,
the bones gather to sing

in an empty ashtray, a deep well,
this lessening of hunger
as the years become sufficient

to themselves. Or am I saying
that white must be perfection,
a clean plate, a light without a source

the failure to remember your smell
a hiding of every colour
memory crying for water.

CARAVANS

The weather is old.
Feathers of words drift
between rains, time
of Ovid watching the Black Sea

wanting home. But that
was his story. The rain
lifts, and someone's face
is watching you, still

for just this moment
without expression, like the sea's edge
where children were playing
only yesterday. Ships

came and went
carrying messages the rain
dissolved. Forgive me, they read.
I am penitent, let me return.

Years pass, but never completely
lose us. Pass like ancient skirts
of dancing bears and caravans
in the mud between rains. Death

was fire and the rains
extinguished it. Never
exile when your own shadow falls
foot by mile by plot along

the weather's old roads.
The words were harsh feathers
that scratched at your throat
in the dust between rains. Dry

not tears. No grief
like old grief settled deep
under the stony earth, deeper than
where rains can loosen it. Bodies

not names. Not histories where
the letters get lost or misread
in lives which were fires until
the rains extinguished them. The

bright skirts and the caravans
passing. The poet crying for his mother
tongue at the sea's edge, not
lost, but found. Between

rains a face you never saw before
watching you try to recognize
yourself. The mirror at the sea's edge
between rains lifts its eyes.

I am drawn to *bèi,* the Chinese cowrie radical
in its simplified form, how it resembles
a hidden man stepping out cautiously
in the shadow of his hood, off to the right
as all characters move to the right
if they move at all. Cowrie shells
were money in ancient China. The figure occurs
in keeping with things of value, commerce, trade.
But I think of him walking the streets alone
night and day, with no thought but to hide himself
like Camus' stranger or Eliot's compound ghost
the masked spirit of some truth whose voice
and silence keep the broken sun from rising
too soon for us, who choose his company.

PISCEAN SONG

I have run away so often
turned my back
I am like the road

I have abandoned so many
places and been left for dead
in houses that went dark

and there are some half-dozen
faces I regret whose names
are holes left in my mind

holes that begin to fill
slowly with dark water
reflecting nothing

though occasionally on clear nights
the stars lean down
they say that memory is time

time now and little else
gone farther and farther away
my mirror that lies to me
my soft voice no one answers

The sea curls and curls
and I am taken away
always from where I have been.

STUMP

The burnt-out house we are always
afraid of. One open
upstairs room made over to the
voices of stars, a song
beyond itself returning to our ears.

In the beginning the shadows of our hands
played with us, the shapes
of light before our bodies could crawl.
I remember the old stump
where the tree was. Darker clothes
that hid my mother's face. The
soft laundry folded by the years.

When we were young
the answers were what we touched.
The grain of words was something less than paper
more than the wind. The rain
brings me to you. The rain that
precedes fire, that soaks the hard dirt road.

We all rise too early
or we sleep too late. The
golden grain we ran through down to the valley
is the texture of a painting. Where the
roof was, where the stars
kill time. I have

trouble now imagining where I belonged
and in what season, whose house this is.
My grandchild's eyes are bright water drops
in the night sky. She is new to us.
We hold to what we have. We hold hold.

RAILROAD TRACKS, HOUSE FOR SALE
AND CLOUDS

She left us while the light was bad.
A sudden movement on the hill, pepper
shaken from heavy clouds.

Someone kept asking, who?
But in a voice I didn't understand
like rain in a dry field, remotest echo.

The sweep of the long field slightly uphill
framed by two eucalyptus in the midground.
SEVENDE ESTACASA. Silence of afternoon.

And the tracks long long ago abandoned.
Grey deliberate rails from left to right
and back again, the eye the only pilgrim.

From left to right and back again
across the high, brown, dry sun-tipped grass.
Like her mind, like that dead tree.

Or the other one fallen on the roof
too frail to break the tiles, or the hill line
beyond, where we saw her move.

And the clouds darkening now,
the fire at their edges softer, gone.
Snow in the Andes. Hail on the lower fields.

How memory brings us to a place
then hides like that, leaving not even a name.
I call and hear nothing but holes.

HAPPINESS

No one goes to the park in winter.
Quiet hands, eyes, there is little to speak of.
Absence is a colour not a sound.

Unless when the sound dies it becomes
the colour white, as in a Chinese story
by Lu Hsun from which the opening line

of this poem comes. There a thin man
a good teacher who lost his job, a misanthrope
who loved only children, died

spitting blood, like a red sound on the snow
white of Chinese death. So this park
where I think the two of us walked once

I've forgotten if we ever came here but
we lived close by, whatever the season was
it returns to me now as a place filled with voices

I thought were ours. I open this book
and the pages turn to leaf and winterbrown grass.
Over it all broods the distant waking sun.

FEBRUARY

I stood on the back deck and then
a jewel of a moon came up and hung
among the branches. They seemed closer now.
I've heard that some with good eyes
can read by moonlight, the faint tracks on the page
like animal whispers but with human meanings.
The light on bare Mediterranean hills
can be like that by day. Whatever moves
has always been there. I know
of no time when a spirit has not been alive
though there can be no proof, only
this longing. That when you are most alone
you are most in love, it is only you can't
touch what it is, hung
above the trees in the light of her
pure being. Whether young or old
it is a time of waiting under thin branches
for the light to clothe itself, the words take leaf.

POSTCARD

If the bodies had all fallen in one place
there could be a place called
Body, a shrine as it were
to the dead of many wars and other griefs

and the sand would not retreat back to the sea
so the sunbathers and swimmers
could live their lives forever watching each other
from that single place in the world

where the sky's white cotton, wet or dry
is rising and sinking along the rim of an arm
whose pale hairs or dark hairs
stir gently in a breath that could be the wind

the wind coming or going, before or after
the life of that place, and the slow roll of the waves
is a hand turning, pleading, explaining
that this is how it starts, and where it ends.

SOFT VOICES

Where they came and fed you in time and you
lived on as their child. They are proud
to have done this, but now after each arrest
the posters on your bedroom walls remind them
your name was only provisional, they'd planned
a better one. You are an old man now

though you don't believe it. The world
out there is so bright, the river shining, the trees
shining like water. You are fed by their hands
who took you as their child, only so nervously
you hardly taste a thing. One or two
leave and return from summer vacations and cruises

bringing you back fresh names. At night the soft sands
keep the impression of your skull, the hair thinned
to strands of distant wind. You are our father.
We plant you here to blossom in your own time
between the cat and the dog, above the red ants
and below the katydids. Seven times the quiet earth

will call to you, men drilling through a solid rock
by the streetcar line will pause, just for a moment.
Is there nothing we can do for you, nothing
your seed gathers to ask. Ann, Joan, Henry, Joe
and the old ones who nurtured you so long ago
who are they, and were they wrong?

THE INTIMACY OF DISTANCE

Someone mentioned the *intimacy of distance*
as if we knew what it meant, how
far I have to go to feel
how close you are.
              But that isn't
what he had in mind. The farther away
the place you long for where you have never been
the deeper inside you it grows
like a human child. But that
was not his point either.
              To love someone he said
you must be content to imagine her.
But to love in that way
is to circle forever the cold point in the eye
at the centre that sees all things but itself.
              He could have meant
there is no satisfaction comes to hand
that the hand can keep. It breaks
like a caught bird, soars, returns to the sky
as a mere colour for air.
              Say blue, say grey.
And yes it vanishes.
And I remember why.

WINTER

Strange prophecies often hide
in rainstorms or under puddles.
Flies in the skull of a deer
making the deer sing.

Over the long fields the teeth of fences
whisper to the ants. I never knew
if you were telling the truth.

As poetry spills over its banks
if spoken too long. As the flooded fields
of late January imagine the sun
as an old man a woman's hand.

The dog sleeps her years
in the leaf pile I raked for her bed.
The future breathes so slowly in the old.

GRANDDAUGHTER

Starting to crawl, she noses to earth
like a mole, it is too hard for her.
She must lie waiting like a seed
until spring when the earth is softer.
No, she is an animal she
can't wait. No says yes and the
arms brace hard and her fingers
dig deeper, the carpet is a field
at night filled with hidden dangers
hunters, shadows, cries. And later
in dreams she will relive this
slow flight through exile, from the
first dark that would claim her again
if it could, straining now
toward the faint horizon of human voices
calling her home, asking her
where have you been, we've waited
a long time, tell us
what it was like back there.

SAN MICHELE, VENICE

To visit the dead you must cross the water
to an island like this
fringed with black cypresses.

The grand words the long silence
of Ezra Pound has come to this
a simple name without dates

on a stone under a tree so hard to find
it took us more than an hour
the name hidden by leaves
the old name covered with dead leaves.

Back in the place he loved
like Odysseus, back to the island
he loved, who spoke with the dead
in harsh words of blood also

a journey done, almost without companions
in the end. And the living city
behind us sinking slowly west with the sun.

FORCE AND SHADOW

The lime after storm light
dulled to olive at the edges of trees
a stillness hung with whispers *place*
I have not taken seriously enough
without wind memory falls
just lies there. One is always

in training and never quite prepared
straining into the silence to hear
another wind, another voice
a red bicycle racing across a blue sea
or from the sky a bird with four black wings
falling, lamenting. So there is

no grief without laughter, my
brave daughters, my mother, father
down the whole line, not hand in hand but
those old pictures. Something passed
hand to hand without hands ever touching
the afternoon rain, the place

momentarily permanent, Neruda's
sad face like a sly gambler's
under a checkered cap, grinning at us.
But it doesn't focus there. The clown
has other business, ways, places to go.
The new moment's movement when it begins
is almost too subtle to catch, the flick
of an eye where force enters shadow
and were you there?

MEMO

The way they walked
who were more to you than others
walking towards or away
depending on the mood or time of year

and how close it was
to the beginning or the end
towards or away
anticipation regret

walked with a slight sway
brown tweed skirt blue shoes
toes pointed outward

fine square shoulders set
face tilted up
or down when brooding

someone to meet
coming towards you
someone to regret
leaving turned away

so is the lyric enough
to make memory happen
the day grey or blue
eyes touched with green

and no background? a long
wide street with trees in leaf
the shadow moving behind
asking no questions.

NEWS FRAGMENT

What dies before it is found
known, accomplishes itself.
Simple chemistry. A baby
covered with ants. Found. Alive.

In the morning the rush of cars
bears me with it into the sun.
Moons my mother drank to keep her figure
fertile. Images never lie.

There are dates I felt the abstract waves of fear
pressing on me like a refusal
to understand. Why probe for chaos
with the tip of a pen, your duty

is naming things. Yes but who
can you name, what far witnesses call
to attend your rebirth? Everywhere the grass
is growing faster, thicker—

it is green by day. It is green
also at night, you believe that.
My enigma was always my absence
I heard you say, *I cast no shadow on things.*

O saint, whoever, cry for the one found
alive. Cry for the small ants that have
only to live. Cry for what is forever being
found and is nameless.

READING LATE

What affections I took to be eyes.
Whatever moves the western sky is blue.
Two cars stopping to talk
beside a long green hedge.
The shadows were deepest blue.

The pages turn so slowly.
In later life you discover another
name for the sun
a word much closer to blood.
An irony.

You are here. You were there.
What I loved
were details in an old stone wall.

And the word *edge*
is sharp, not soft. You think
of soft edges, but the words don't meet.
The way her legs swam uphill
in the dry mountain air. And her shoes

like two cars talking
by a long green hedge
until someone yells "Goodbye."

The dark of the western sky.
The western sky is always hungry.
It feeds on the creatures it dreams.
Such ironies I took to be
signs of life.

ILLEGALS

Another killing along the river.
Soap makes the hands clean, a clear
mirror reflects what looks like eyes.

Mother I'm thirsty, said the first child.
Then the necklace broke and her children fell,
scattered. Pity the man with the gun

who has to take care of us. I was
born with legs to run and hands
to ward off evil. To work the dust

into shapes of men and women and sell
for money. A brown-eyed man with a
blue-eyed job he is trained not to hate

saw my reflection and fired. The mothers
wait all their lives for death, so as not
to see death again. But it comes

as a mosquito comes, small, a thin sound.
The brown river runs between our fingers.
The masks we wear to hide us are the sun.

FRIDAY THIRTEENTH

In the sea the river
drowns. No one has opened this door
for years, the latch has stuck.

Shadowy eyes of dogs
linger in the pitfalls of your dreams.
Who was the woman the woman the one

who wept for you? Crazy garbage
scattered outside, frozen beyond its smell.

Old wooden houses of the old.
Where I imagine I am
they speak no language. The snows

came and went, generations of names
under a roof of sod: into the sunlit
nursery where you felt at peace with light
until the light closed your eyes

and my memory. How old are you now?
I have learned how to form my capitals
and punctuate my sentences. It is

the scream I can't quite control
as the wind can never be silent. Turn

from the beginning to the end
and read it all backward. Ignore
the in-between which is forever where you are.

I have a face for you.
Do you have eyes for me? Eyes
the philosopher said, can only smile in a face
which is the frame of sky where

birds fly. But you began to speak
of the river and the sea. You began
telling me something. Is it where

pain touches us? Give me time
to open your letter and read it.
Somewhere along the trail of sand between words

cities are named, and children. Pauses
where water gathers. Long
winters spent asleep on the smoky ovens
of other ancestries, staying

alive. If a bird flies in
it has lost its way. Keep asking what I meant.

The rain that touched this house.
The roof above it and the stone-grey sky.
All things too simple to know.

TERRITORY

Extravagant under mountains
in the heads of mice
brown mice, grey mice, dogs
axles stuttering through the load of mud

as if borders are what lie beyond the eyes'
peripheries, nowhere more to go, no
start or finish, to wake with nothing in mind
on the rainiest of April Saturdays

at home in the old house
thunder breaking, cold, the dog wanting in
and after a last word with the self who went
his own way years ago and lives up there

in high mountains beyond the rain
in winds beyond the mountains, in such cold
he breaks sticks to make fires, and denies
he was ever my brother

this language that leaves in time
a mothlike dust, a faint powder of lives
fluttering like memory at the womb—
what was it gave the sun so many names

and in the intellect a flame still as glass
hard as this pebble I found.

GERNIKA

All night a thing
on a distant string...

The revolution must begin
in our hearts.

We who know how to use time
will prevent it

this time. O Mother
who stole your milk from us.

Madrid, May 2001

WINTER GRASS ON THE PLAINS

The beach where whoever's footprints made it in
was it Amelia or some castaway, they
found so little. At that edge
where life is always beginning, starting over
as if it had never happened: a ship's
broken wheel or the long wheel of a wagon
missing one spoke—into that gap crawls
an idea like a legend. Where spread is so wide
that nothing is tall enough to be vertical
then who can find you. I miss
myself. I miss the memory of you there
in the other room, in the far part of the house
that keeps its own night and day, its
weather, hours, directions. Out there
on the rim of the sea, at the edge of the cattle pond
the silvery grass shines under low dark cloud
and this is what the searchers found when they came
expecting nothing they could call their own.

LATE NIGHT MOVIE

What air can you collect that you won't
match me grain for grain to say my prayers
a window, say, the long sparse light
opposite for hundreds of miles, a land
rolling and characterless except for the TV screen
where a man and a woman shape their love
to fit the pattern we are willing to bear
as extras, all of us. I have in mind
a spirit that won't refuse, being foolish, to run
the beautiful eyes of the visionary or saint
whose cold shadow walks past him
counting all his moments without a name
under the long sun: to prepare his place
in the absence of any party further to this
which is anywhere anywhere now
you name the place we'll build the town around it
this is the man this is the woman. These ones.

WILD EYES

I have set plaster to catch a foot.
Who is the runner who passes every day
                leaving nothing behind him.

As the rains begin
autumn is still a ghost
or an unborn child waiting to name its mother.

Headaches and the rain!
In mourning for his dog the poet wrote
                dog a thousand times.

At three in the morning the sun is too close.
How can I organize the events
that led me here.

                Where

is the money. What time did the train leave
bearing away my sins
the memory of my father ending with me.

FRICTIONS

A man running on a background of wind
among graves. Where is the suit
on the empty hanger. How long
can I play.

The picture of a heart done in blue crayon
on white paper. Somewhere
they exchanged eyes.

A man running in an unlucky direction
calling out to someone. The light is against him.

The light is in his eyes
as the trees turn the leaves burn.

As the leaves fall *fric fric*
on the dry pavement. How far can he run
calling calling against the hurt light
his hands reversed
his head and feet

reversed. The coat hanger and the man
are both naked. Something

fell on the roof. Something
falls on the roof
where the house stood.

This is a painting about a change of season
a change of heart affecting the mind of light.

So little time to notice little things.

HOW THE ELDERLY ARE BORN

I heard them speak of the *elegance of rain*
in the brown slum garden. The old
had wooden hands. They clicked their fingers
and I caught the soft voice of Lupe Salcedo:
"I have no animosity towards my lovers
only hate." And the shutter fell
and cut them off at the neck. Though
they had done nothing wrong but wandered
into the wrong frame, like inadmissible memories
that won't let go, evidence of lost time
or time one must face among strangers. No one
knows me here. I take my life in my hands
that open and close like an overdue book
of hours so personal there are no signs.

SUNLIGHT THROUGH BLINDS,
FOUR O'CLOCK, FACING WEST

Whoever comes stepping through the frame
make it worthwhile for us now.
Beyond the trees there is a river
and beyond that a dark headland
knifed by the prow of a long canoe
forever still in its movement.
And my eyes fail, and give back
whatever it was they saw
whatever it was they understood they saw
for it is blank now. I go to live
in some future of memory among
the howls of the skins of dead animals
who spread their soft-eyed bones
over mountains and plains and through towns
where the light picks us up and walks us home.

BETHLEHEM

The late-night light that accompanies
the companionless, the white
neon light no one can turn off
god knows how many miles between towns
as quiet as this one.
                          When the child is born
it will have visitors. The first to come
they shall be holy.
                          What did she think
when they asked her name and her husband's
business there, whispering to themselves
until daylight put out the light.
What do they dream in the dark
when the wind brings a baby in its mouth.

INCARNATIONS

Every fart begins
as a breath of fresh air

A dry old man
who talks to himself
and to animals

He would twist the sun if he could
Wring it out
Eat it as bread. Eat

Corn Woman said. But
If you forget to think of me
or make use of me
without remembering my words

And Dawn the tawny one
doe bloodied by the arrow that pierced
her father in their lovemaking

Her sadness will spread too
to the other animals

To write my empty page
in this book that others have written

As a bird watches
another eating
a berry

Eyes eyes everywhere always
No way out of it

Three dogs tossing a cat
until it is only a skin filled with blood
Watch and do nothing

In the beginning
is always something
that later gets hidden

The burden of a poem is its own
lightness. Who can hear
me

Rustle of ants carrying leaf-bits
to their nest at the earth's centre
Eyes of danger

To write and fill my page
with emptiness

Though nature compensates
A man born without eyes
might have two assholes

Dry old man
Dry twigs rubbed together
Happiness that is born
not of desire

He is the shadow that precedes
the body

comes and goes

as fire goes home
withdraws to its dark house

Silence
is a part of speech

You kneel
And then you are free.

IT HAPPENS

A house's perfect time is when
the frame is up, not yet the roof and siding.
The young wood is still warm to the touch.
You feel the grace and tension of the bones.

Later there will be shadows. Lives
clothed in lives. Rooms filled
and rooms to spare, the crying aloud
of love and birth and death. Young wood grown old.

I have made this happen too fast
too suddenly. In between is where things gather
to wear their masks and dance their winter spring

with a fine sense of occasion. Time
is forever on our side. Who would believe
the face in the old hall glass still bears your name.

WATERMARKS

I

The dog trots up to sniff the tree
The dog trots back again

The dog trots up to sniff the tree
The dog trots back again

The dog trots up to sniff the tree
The dog trots back again

The tree waits

II

Blue waits in you
as a dream waited behind the sun.

American man
is a son of a gun.

The wheat field weaves
spiders who are thin men.

III

A man turns round and round
on the street corner. Something
he can't find or is trying to
complete, in himself
or around himself. His feet

own nothing but
the circles he makes. The deep
city around him siphons off noise
like a time-funnel. Earth

is extra. Earth is a
ring of bones. When in time I'm asked
to greet the stranger whose suit is worn
from mere rain and the sun. He
does not resemble my father, or yours.

APPLES AND APPLES

When she was a girl in Palestine
a soldier made her promises.

The wind off the sea
was a hand caressing her back—

inland the windblown sand
bit deep as bone.

I came upon her early.
She came upon me late.

Or put it another way, she had
lived more, longer, passionately afraid

where I was timid. Seven years between us.
Seven planets, seven stones smeared with blood.

We were both wanderers. But
she'd had to learn to live in ways

where I was innocent, death
in Europe had been real. For her

the subterfuge of languages.
For me the words we shared.

Too early and too late
can't average out as just in time.

Apples and apples. A door open
is always just closing.

No joy there now, no grief.
Fierce numbers feed the stars.

NOCTURNE

House like a restless sleeper
shifts here
           settles there
suddenly
doors don't fit

Mother swift feeding her young
drops too far down the chimney
           out the flue
flits from room to room
           wall window door
fighting the dark
a fact
brushing a dream

Awake now
now not
image of arctic sun
           all night
around the eye's horizon
circling

           animal
gentle or fierce
pure wonder
           in this house
fitted to my bones

Through trees the follow-through
of night wind asking birds
           hello the screech owl calls
closer to time

far wheels driving hard
around dangerous curves
                the old road
        even at this hour
who's coming home

Father why are you
waiting for me
                your train left
almost thirty years ago
on rails of fire
                in winter
ashes to earth
where mother went first

Tomorrow a blank page
tonight a poem
the furnace where seeds of words
                melt and cry
wanting lives
wanting mouths

to kiss
to speak
                I breathe
grateful to hear the birds.

CALL NOTES

I looked over the long valley
before I started down
acres and acres of other people's
strangeness—
roofs, cars, a barn, children running—

what time was it
the colours I wanted to touch
this angle, that flatness

like coming home, but
the smell of others' cleanliness
a faint cry from the white house
a name just a sound—

there, there, running—
a girl's dress red as poppies
catching the sun

the long valley a face facing a face
facing it
in sudden time

the windy place you come to—

IMPRESSION

Quiet, and the hill settles
toward light, makes
this less difficult.

In the dark you were a figure of dream
eyes come gone a figure of laughter
mocking us. The clock
we fear is only our own waking

as the numbers rise.
Days nights sun and moon
the numbers. The clock
is my mouth.

Overland they come in wagons
making no noise. Their names
are a long paper sheet of wind

and if I am their son or was their father
you are what else to me? The rocks
never spoke. The water
rose up high then fell and dried to powder.

I have done these things well
those things badly.
You come to me now asking for more.

*As long as the grass shall grow
or the waters run* they promised.
The skull I found is abuzz with memories
or words that are memories

as if the fears I took to be yours
were mine all along. Curved
like seashells or old swords
or bamboo in the rain, bent

to earth like a sheltering mother.
In the dark when you came you were
a light. But the coming of light

killed you. Light
which is everywhere but not at once, your
face changes, your eyes soften, harden, die.

One of us is wrong.
Who. The other. Now
daybreak, now noon. Who
gave us these names.

LUCKY NUMBERS

I

I dream sometimes
we meet
and there is regret
that after all
the chances
there was no chance.

But trouble
in someone's life
after which
the sand keeps falling

and the sun
seen through smoky glass

only unnerves the dark
does not detain it

long. White against black
in formal squares along a winter path.
White air. Crack of thunder or bone.

II

Where nothing walks are shadows
of other things. Trees. A broken fence.
A pot of flowers. That tank
hidden under branches of veins.

What do I know which year.
A hand of cards, fanned, held close.

A wine-stained wooden table
the rain raining outside

months of patient waiting
someone's child by the hand.

III

Who are the refugees?
Where have they hidden their eyes?

Your uncle has a weak fart.
He will die.

Then let the wind
carry his whisper off
to the ant queen's nest

before winter comes—

I bear no man a grudge.
I speak because I'm spoken to.
When my smell dies
another smell revives
to take its place.

Blue, yellow, red
what flower are you?

OF MAGIC

Because she was always dusty and dirty, they called her
Cinderella. Light of my tired eye. Who was a father left thus
where the light fell dead. Or music emptied of sound, just a
tremor, like a far-off eye watching unseen. When the prince
came he had a bad limp. Things change, there is nothing to
be said that hasn't already been described, over and over
again, in the way words have of startling into life like a
herd of grazing deer panicked by someone's footstep. Has
he come? Yes, but that is not the one I dreamt would come.
Hand me the broom. Tonight is overtime.

NOT THERE YET, NOWHERE NEAR

Morning. Across the hills
cistercian rain, a thousand-year-old
silence.
                    Eyes (Wittgenstein)
can only smile
in a face. What you would be or do
after it ends.

When it said its voice I said no this is
arithmetic, stop counting.
Silence. Music. Give me time to go
where the light is.

Red, yellow, blue
the cardinal colours.
Three the perfect number. No
fish, flesh or eggs.

Great Horned Owl and I are awake
his eight-syllable call
with a pause in the middle
                    the downward glide
on the last note
like a child's complaint. I'm hungry.

Morning a grey feather.
Moderation of rain, whisper of
old prayer. Cultivated hunger
in the gardens of wind.

And the news.
Police searched the school.
A robot blew up a backpack.
Nothing was found.

LIFELINES

Placenta
abandoned on an anthill.
Lives I have left.

To feed with my hands
my mouth, your body
my blood, finger by
finger loosening.

Lives I have left
behind. Red and brown
the paired cardinals
sing into the tempo of the sun

—mistakes my hands make
choosing words. Future
loosens like soil around an old root.

And I have avoided your graves
as well as I could,
the precise hour or place
my obligation.

The burnt photos and the letters gone
are like old hunger, eaten alive.
When someone asks my name I give your names.

Late May, black pieces of sun
circle on wings overhead.
The smell of spring earth

is perfect. Mother
you come to me always as rain.
I have had no victories.

The other dead
will not go away.
No one will let them
go, I live in silence.

In knowledge, in ignorance.
What can I say will be heard.
We who parted company

so long ago knew only
what we were. The curse
of poetry is this desire for beauty
where none survives. Only

questions, ashes. There are
no favourite poems. Dead spiderlegs,
a dried moth by the window, time.

I burn you now
and in burning you
myself. The mouths of ants
cut cleanly as fire.

HIGH WINDS AND HEAVY SNOWS

When you look up
from your book
so suddenly—

having remembered nothing
of the last ten pages

but your absence of mind—
the words were strangers
in a foreign city, one

familiar to you only in dreams
where a voiceless thought tells you
this is *here, that* is where you are

and each native like each snowflake has a face
and the wind they speak is untranslatable—

a look in your eyes so lost
you could be anywhere at any time—

and I hide my face
not wanting to be found.

MEMO

Who does not want my child
may not have her

the long tongue of thirty years
I find dry pavement
here is the word you sing

like sunlight indefinite
to be trusted not loved
to be loved but not trusted

like ancient rain
to be drunk by small degrees
as dry words

and where have they buried us
who put the squirrels to dig here
looking for names

these are particulars
there is no ledger only the sound of wind

oleander in a valley in Spain
below the broken goat corral
much later

mother daughter together
think together think
of time as like the feathers of a bird

clutching what can't be kept
the air his eyes
looking elsewhere away

here are words for you
that stone won't take
they are not strong enough

there is no apt photograph
no faithful likeness

now you are free to live.

THE COLOUR OF ROCKS, OF BREAD

can live where there are stories
blue in the depth of a pail
someone's old paint

A human face
always appears to be waiting
some sudden knowledge

and the desert appears to be shallow
because there are few shadows
Where light is everywhere
who touches what

And can a finger claim
it has that experience
I was there I felt you move

If that season could return
always appears to be waiting
the certainty there's nothing more
a hand can say

a hand burnt onto cement
a human profile photographed
on white rock

ancholia the columbine
flower of sadness some
of madness others

But the best bread talks to you
You live it as you eat it
a messenger thirsting for breath
at the end of his hot race
against time

heat/cold

muscat grapes
laid out to dry as raisins in the sun
the few dry facts that stand between
a life or a death sentence

As the desert is finally home
It is your shadow I fail to see
so far away so bright my eyes fail.

ANSWERS

What is the time of day
listening in a stone
warmed in an old woman's hand
on a concrete bench
in a square in an old town

a name older than mine
though grass drifts in the air
at the same instant I hear
the wind blow her skirt from black to shadow
like weather changing

when we return from war
when they returned from wars
the garden was always there waiting
though the postcards have turned brown
a dog's jaw buried to help

corn or alfalfa grow
a superhighway crosses the bridge
that connects time as it joins
both shores that long ago were one
was it her dog her garden

her son who didn't return
is she Dolores or Maria
or Kristen Helen Angelique
waiting for the sun to marry the wind
like weather turning

a name older than the town
an older name than any town
the square the fountain named for who
first put it there
no clock heard anywhere

to what lover she gave birth
who drank her wine and left her dry
the wind to blow it all away
as footsteps up the rocky path
the stone drops from my hand.

MASTER OF WIND

I was not quick enough
or too quick, and you hadn't moved.

Into my hands fell the old air
of paint on canvas, indoor words
settling like flies.

One century then another
stirred the calendar. My hands

opened and closed. *I am*
so sorry I can't be there
our lives take time —

memory split in half
like silence in old wood—

cries, thrown on the flame.
And you hear your birth over and over again
in the spring grass.

One of us here.
One of us there.

VANISHED NUMBERS

The shops are closed
      light finds other shadows

in that face
a crooked sign
      a night lit with rain

that memory is all breath can spare
for imagining   one sign or two
to open

virtualities
a hand banging metal   is it Cain
the blacksmith
          no stranger now

marked by fire

One goes   then two   ten
that the race survive   or that it die

night wet with such light
no name   no place   no tokens
the rain a kind of dignity
        thin wash of milk

into whatever's face lifts gazing up
with no reason to count or hope

City   City of ours
O night of
        hidden answers
                vanished numbers

leaf   arrow   vein.

SEED, LIGHT

Singularly where the sky walks
the flight of a bird
                hand-me-down
to wrestle with nothing
is to have no strength

but the wind is not nothing
you can avoid
                though not know
backwash of intellect
moving the river
                to and fro
the way coitus might happen

I would like to begin
        I would have liked to begin
owning nothing
but my beginning

not star nor telescope
walking the light of my seed
        up, into the infinities of touch

in the cold air
no angel
given my name.

FUGITIVES

A man turning his back
shot while attempting to escape
white peasant cotton, wide hat.

Why this dream now
while the light bends slowly up through the trees
on panther feet. I must
organize. Age is like the light

crossing slowly. In there are bodies
I never knew, eyes, fingernails,
an amplitude of names caressing themselves

desiring others. The man
falls, and there are holes of blood
spreading over the continent. Nothing
cries in the early heat where dust is cover.

That was long ago. Though dreams
welcome men who would escape, and the women
who come to understand, who always

understood. I keep my word; I hide
him and feed him, blot his wounds.
I open my eyes now watching

the trees bend in the wind, while over the grass
on hands and knees come shadows
and syllables of light, the young
helping the old along until they become air.

MAN CARRYING A SUITCASE

There is a time
under the river
fish swim with such grace

a shadow to catch
a shadow disembarking from
an escalator of wind

crying someone's name
in time to catch the taxi
of his life—

alone as the body
always is itself
resembling no one

though names come to mind
names like numbers
running on two legs

in someone's mind—
the catastrophe of keeping
up with things

across the floor
out through the portal of light
between this shore and that

a flash of anonymous love
someone not important
where do they go.

EYES

The last buddha was lost
in one of our moves

what you don't look after
someone takes
so life changes, and lives change

and in the end do you care
what you have and are
so many things wander out there
nameless as snow or rain

hands looking to reach
anything more solid than mere touch
a word, a parable

her profile on a transatlantic ship
looking out to sea, which is nowhere
what remains when the eyes go
eyes, that is, of memory

the accuser and pardoner
the one you can never trust
but call your father

dry old man who must go
and you must follow

not quite, because her face
is never the same
her womb an acorn or a maple seed
or a garden where deer walk

step by step
like a thing coming to mind
a memory, or its forfeiting

to desire, a different opening
or ending, mice
lost in the sun, field mice
alive under the snow

her profile becoming eyes
that look at you
another year when the sea
that year when the sea

on blank days
they look down from windows
as if watching for you to come home

but you have moved so often
you could be anyone.

DEPARTURES

They hung
stations from her eyelids
with real trains—
Anna, or
whoever takes her place.

Across the wind-darkened harbour water
white sails. Mud and rain
tracked in on children's feet.
Where, where have you been?

The lonesome train of her heavy century
long gone. Explosions still to come.
For me, a silence
in my ears, a winter
haiku—

Shimogyo ya
yuki tsumu ue no
yoru no ame

> *In the lower town*
> *across the heaped-up snow,*
> *whisper of night rain*

One is so frail.
Two are hardly better.
They were jackhammering the street outside
a day before the news came.

I like to think the snow
will give her back her shadow.
Milk across darkening grass, the cold.
Daphne gone to tree,
doe-ears flicking.

HISTORIES

It was another country
and none of us understood
the mission of the conquerors
was to lose themselves

lose themselves, and find
what someone else had named
before they came
in words they could never pronounce
sounds muffled to the tongue

like bones, woman bones
had yours not burnt to ash
words muffled to the tongue
father mother love

such fierce life this new world
they came to enslaved
by their age-blackened sun
dream of a golden wilderness

your missing letters to me
my ones to you I burnt
to an ash whiter than bones
because the voice I found there
was that of a frightened child

mine, but not mine. Now this
memory of our lives
and how the conquest took us
takers, taken, one by one.

Were we a people a place
or was the hair teeth eyes
made into masks, given names
the painted masks of clowns

who live in comedies how people
come to grief, rise
and grace us with tears and words
a history that won't end

no jesus no nails of blood
no mission no cross no
blessed name of mary
to see us through

the deceit of poetry
the astonishment of a death without
angels the long still lines
who wait under theater marquees
silent in the cold spring rain.

WIND

There's a loud word for it
and a soft word. It is not

everywhere, but somewheres
and while it is there

is everything. Deep song
the thumb strums

can fill the heart. Let
this anger between us end—

a mirror can wake the sun
like nothing on earth.

We are blessings all of us.
We scatter like air.

NEW YEAR

First day, writing into the grey
morning silence
                as through falling snow
my daughters my son.

He said, I have stories to tell you.
If the words taste bitter they're mine.

But it is another year. The wind
opens leafless mouths in the trees
not song but wind.
                Shan Silver Ana Matt
such distances those Indian ponies crossed
riding away, their backs turned
to ourselves who are not there.

Who are you where are you going?
Hard to hold you still
bring you close.

A story that asks for help
as in the African picture-word
I lift you from the river
with my hands
                But I say no

I'm not the one
you think, the story-man
try there, try
the internet, look there
where must be helpful hands.

I light my fire for you
with paper words. Winter is cold.
In January oak leaves still fall
on the north wind, old
boyhood omen, friend.

Come play. Come play
as what struggles there
in the deepening snowflake.

You had a friend and a time.

Grey to pale half-white as the sky
red dots in the distance meaning
a name forming

a body coming home.

CAT AND MOUSE

What does a poem want?
Huts without doors
and blind children peering.

More than a measure of rain.
Air that blows in and out of lives
promising, threatening. To
close the door on eyes that have no language

like a wandering comma
in a line of words. Who
witnessed my birth, or yours, that
what isn't fair might be acceptable

at last. So somewhere
something gives, breaks.
I am my own understood.

In the woods below the house vultures settle
in the winter-bare elm tops
(how many, why there)
is a story waiting, some tale

with a sun and a moon
and whatever stars the universe can lend
to outwait this winter. A woman
who knew she must die, but would risk that

because. Whose birth
was irreplaceable. What have you done
to identify the question in your mind

like a lathe turning, like metal wailing.
Cat's eyes watch me from the deck outside
her coat fluffed for the cold. Always
one imagines wind

in the stillest of air. Soft feet
padding along the sky
children of thunder. And would the truth

truly be interesting?
Whose habit do you break
when you break silence?
What must be said for whose sake—

like naming a stone
then throwing it away.
"Old friend…" the letter begins
or might have.

A poem watches with big eyes
like children startled in a doorless yard
no grass just dust. As if

silence ever was. I am
the record of something never said, it says.
Watch as the light turns my way.
It is the mask of the sun.

LIGHTS ACROSS THE LAKE

Who's memorable is what water answers
reflectively, the first date

that failed for want of experience
as must have happened in that scented garden

where fruit hung heavy and fell.

Nothing survives stupidity.

One summer at a time goes dark.
The vigil of old eyes

turns on itself. No reason to mourn
what was never there, a touch

that began and ended at the
same moment. Except now looking across

the darkened lake of fifty years
something naked swims close, with her eyes

a wavelet
breaks at my feet.

SCATTERING

Brother and sister
the light turns their way.

Outside, sun covers the snow.
No time. No wind.

In the light
they look thin.

          ❧

Distress is what focuses the eyes.
Something, a
disturbance, panic, angels.

The last time I was home
it wasn't there.

          ❧

You are half the time what I'm not ever.
Where it went wrong
enough for us to see.

The holy ghost is, what, an ancestor.
God help that in our hands.

My shadow moves
slowly across the clockface
like a third eye.

No, the third eye's finger
probing every place
the circle wants to stop.

𝄐

Ouch for chrissakes that was my head.
Give me time with your ghost.

I am only
inches ahead of you. Give me

your hand. One or
other of us will be born

tonight.

𝄐

Tomorrow
becomes today. Two
figures backlit by a rising moon

are turned which way
the light
or the risen dark.

Struggling to be reasonable.
The cold helps.

What I turn into

unmasks I am

with no bitterness.

&

You were passionate once
and called things by their names
listening for the echo
of your name. Whoever
did this needs to know that.

&

I step on my shadow
searching for yours. The lost

penny I pick up
brings the thought of luck, it

might have been yours, or if
the stranger cared. One

loses what another finds.

&

I imagine the Cross
as a garden filled with wind.

Two people meet there, calling to a third
who never comes.

Light falls evenly on all the stones.

What matters is to see the picture form.

No otherwise.

TIME OUT

Out there, rain telling the trees
to repeat their leaves

Father, you are the shadow
I stepped from

You I haven't talked to for years
bear with me

Out there, the rain
saying nothing but rain

saying this.

GATHERING

My brother came to me
asking for water.
I said, this is Mother's glass
it is empty now.
He drank, and I drank.
My breath remains.

    ℘

How can I speak of giving.
Leafy spring comes out
to tease us into trusting it.
Another life, it says, another
life. When the killing ends
in Ramallah—but whose
hands can lift the dead
with the absolution of stones.

    ℘

We talked of nothing else
but how hungry we were.
Like cattle with noses forever
to the grass, bent that way
at sunset. Not one looked up
to see the sky we saw.
But their heaven was green.
Their eyes were home.

    ℘

The young painters,
young in their colours.
Had we been
bewildered then? Walking
10,000 invisible steps later
the reds of inflamed eyes
green of a rainy afternoon
in the almost empty gallery
darkening the years back
to where they started from.

&

"You are too serious."
Then let's forget I said that.
"Oh no, just say it again
with a smile."
I smiled and said it again.
And saw it was a lie.

&

A father goes without saying.
A mother would like to fill all
the silences with that look she has.
Time can remember
only what the children say.
Look, learn silence from their eyes.

&

My brother came to me
asking for water.
I said, this is Father's glass
it is empty now.
He drank, and I drank.
My breath remains.

VEGETATION

I

Was awakened by my body uttering
strange syllables; a conspiracy of ants
or politicos from some terror making plans
that concerned us all. I'd dreamed
of my children, of cats pretending to be
my wives, and the air had a smell
of ancestries beyond my memory.
Then the sun opened the room
and some name kept telling me its child
whose cries were redbirds in the cedars.
These are the messengers you live with
by day, and become, at night, if lucky
your old self. I can never remember
why I say *myself* reluctantly.

II

The great hackberry
at the top of the drive
half dead, half green
comes into spring now
like an old woman
whose memory is gone
where green lives bud again
from the living half
whose dead half clings to it
having nowhere to go

keeping the form of the tree's
whole grace intact, sun, rain

the same messenger now
no telling how or when.

III

Rain, rain again. If
I were grass I'd be happy.
Where memory rests…The slow
trickle of water, long
husbanding undertow that keeps sanity
fresh. Nothing to hide from.
All that is is here
the voice says, what you fear
has already happened. Wait
until the rain makes eyes
that look at you directly.
There are no honest mirrors.
I say *eyes*, *eyes* as though
the eyes were my own.

SPRING 2001

Where was there what time
Is where we begin…
Collect again what scattered

come, go, came, went
an order of verbs
too close to the fingertips
slips out is gone

fragment of a Mediterranean coastline
with blue-white villas   on sand
behind the closed concession stand
a pair of shoes
left waiting   it's no go

out of humour
out of touch

and comes the spring wind
a time for booking journeys
making time
walk ahead on its own feet

warm-green smell soft wind
confusion of waking dreams
lost in some city   gone
if our voices weren't
angry   time

bad and good
in whichever order
my sister, we
survivors, old ones now
ourselves

we, us
taught her 35-year-old parrot
to sing the "Ave Maria" along with her
the sweet and raw voice

mingling   confused in the sun
where was there
that time

March-month   I was your son
I know your wind
that strip of gentle coast where others
always lived   paper, sand

the scattered pieces
I collect
myself.

BOOK CLOSING

The last guests fetch their coats
and walk off home. Turning autumn
their shadows enter night.

Lights on the steep hill far left.
Whiff of coal, tobacco smoke.
Words thinning to air, air dies.

Did you learn why they couldn't see you
thinking you invisible like
the dead in their graves? Were they

the first friends, who lived until sunrise
and opened life and death for you
like an old book, a stream of numbers

voices, riffling on, beyond? *He will grow
tired of me*, she said. *Sleep*, and went
silent. The page writes itself.

Now they are all gone.
Scorpion, bull, lion. And
the little one, a pisces, like these hands.

SOLO WITH GRAZING DEER

Mother's son, father's son.
Late spring, the rain hangs on
like lost sleep.

A smell of fresh soap
when the wind drops. In the field below
a horse neighs. The wet cedars

bend to earth, looking for their roots.
Waxwings tilt and soften
the grey air between branches.

Memories still to come
like waves that haven't yet happened
gazing out across the wall of sea

to where the sea ends. The deer
gone. Myself I've been saying goodbye to
all my life. Beads of rain

like a series of clear names
run together. One, then a
thousand. Then the whole sea boiling.

THE NAMING OF ABSENCE

When I drip ink on a white page
it is morning. Wet or dry
are the shadows around eyes
that walk slowly toward the past

looking for the signs that filled with water
something lost and always something found
a button or a broken comb
not that. You are unlovable

says the grammar of fingers
tapping out the keys the wind dictates
like notes of a song. The
voice of an adjective, the noun's face

streaming in the muted lights of rain—
what is meaning—I can tell you
I was there, as I am here, and the light talks to me
in the voice of an injured animal

accusing the night of being dark
the day not sufficient to heal her.
Where are you going with your hands raised like that?
The day barely begun, and there are cries

happy cries
from the village square. Dreams
that condemned the night to the darkest of blues
drain from the hand basin and leave me

empty of thoughts. The naming
of absence begins in the need to love
what can't be touched: as that
in the middle distance, memory of someone

stripped or clothed, in a field between two trees
is looking away across a distant fence
of calling, or silent. Beyond the subdivision
dies the prairie. I'm inclined to wonder

why I waited so long and no one, nothing—
leaves are falling. What is memorable
must have lived one time, along
the edge of a river or a line of railings

painted fresh black. One hand can touch
so much emptiness. You came away
one afternoon on the late train south
and we crossed the strait and spent two days and nights

at an old hotel, understanding
the time was ours. I think of my childhood
all the years since as being these days
coming as they did to warn us of mornings

later, without eyes. I've given
each of my fingers a secret name, its own
name and memory. The pages of the book
keep turning, and so many are empty.

Notes on Poems

"Railroad Tracks, House for Sale and Clouds." Title of a postcard I picked up in Quito, Ecuador.

"Incarnations." Most of the italicized lines are quotes from Roberto Calasso's fascinating exploration and retelling of the ancient myths of India, *Ka*. Corn Woman is Native American.

"Apples and Apples." Palestine here is the British Protectorate of the 1930's and 40's. The "she" of the poem and her family found haven there from European Fascism.

"The Colour of Rocks, of Bread." In her discussion of Nerval's sonnet "El Desdichado," Julia Kristeva notes that "ancholie" (an ingredient of "melancholie") is French for the columbine flower, and this found its way into my poem. By chance, a few days after I'd finished the poem, the shootings occurred at Columbine High School in Colorado.

"Departures." The winter haiku is by Boncho, a friend and younger contemporary of Basho. Reading it triggered a childhood memory.

"New Year." 'I lift you from the river with my hands' is my interpretation of the pictograph meaning "help" (from *Indaba, My Children*, by Vusamazulu Credo Mutwa).

Acknowledgements

Some of these poems have appeared in *Exile*, Volumes 21.1, 23.2, and 24.4. Others have appeared in *Border- lands*, Number 12, and *The Texas Observer*. The poem "Apples and Apples" was chosen to be part of the poetry project at the 2001 Venice Biennale.

MEMBER OF SCABRINI MEDIA

Quebec, Canada
2001